careers in
TRUCKING

Mark Lerner

photographs by
Milton J. Blumenfeld

Lerner Publications Company
Minneapolis, Minnesota

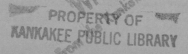

LIBRARY OF CONGRESS CATALOGING IN PUBLICATION DATA

Lerner, Mark
Careers in trucking.

(An Early Career Book)
SUMMARY: An introduction to career opportunities
in the trucking industry, such as warehouse manager, packer,
driver, dispatcher, estimator, mechanic, and purchasing director.

1. Transportation, Automotive—Freight—Vocational
guidance—Juvenile literature. [1. Trucks—Freight—Vocational
guidance. 2. Truck driving—Vocational guidance. 3. Vocational
guidance] I. Blumenfeld, Milton J. II. Title.

HE5611.L37 1979   388.3'24'023   79-18675
ISBN 0-8225-0341-7

International Standard Book Number: 0-8225-0341-7   Library of Congress Catalog Card Number: 79-18675

1 2 3 4 5 6 7 8 9 10 85 84 83 82 81 80 79

Would you like to work in the trucking industry?

Every day, *goods*, or things of value, are moved from one place to another. The trucking industry works to move goods as safely and quickly as possible. To move them, trucks travel great distances—from town to town, state to state, or country to country. Trucks also carry goods between places in the same city.

It takes many people to move goods safely and carefully. The goods may be as large as cars, as heavy as cattle, or as fragile as mirrors. In this book you will read about some of the jobs that these people do. Perhaps you will find one that you would like to do, too.

WAREHOUSE MANAGER

The warehouse manager is in charge of everything in the trucking company's *warehouse*, or storage building. Goods are kept there before they are moved. And when goods come from overseas, they often go first to a trucking company's warehouse. From there, they are delivered to the people who bought them.

The warehouse manager organizes the trucking company's warehouse. He or she knows where everything is. The warehouse manager keeps good records of everything that comes into the warehouse. He or she also writes down the date that goods arrive and leave.

The warehouse manager must make good use of all warehouse space. In this picture, the warehouse manager is using a *forklift* to stack crates closely together.

PACKER

Packers are the workers who pack goods into boxes for moving. Packers must be careful. If they pack something too tightly, it might break. Fragile things, like lamps and plates, are packed with extra care.

Packers use different kinds of boxes to pack different things. Some boxes, like those used for glasses and dishes, are thicker than others. Packers decide which box is best for each thing that must be packed.

When loading trucks, packers put heavier things on the bottom and lighter things on the top. Loading a truck is like putting a puzzle together. Everything that goes into the truck must be packed to fit just right.

EXPORT PACKER

Export packers pack goods for shipment overseas. They pack goods that will travel first by truck and then by ship or airplane. Since the goods usually go a great distance, export packers must pack them in a special way. Export packers often make the crates they send goods in. These crates have to be very strong.

In the warehouses, where they almost always work, export packers weigh and keep records of everything they pack. There they have all the materials that they need—like wood and nails—to get the crates ready for their long journeys.

HELPER

Helpers work closely with packers. But while packers often work in the warehouse, helpers almost always work at people's homes. There they put people's belongings into boxes and carry them to the truck outside. Inside the truck, helpers stack everything. They know just where everything should go.

Helpers must be strong to carry all those boxes. They know that they have done their job well when the things they have packed get to their destination without breaking.

OVER-THE-ROAD DRIVER

Over-the-road drivers *transport*, or carry, goods from one place to another. To do this, they may have to travel long distances. Over-the-road drivers know the country well. They must know which roads are best and which ones are unsafe or are being repaired.

Over-the-road drivers must, of course, be able to drive well. They may have to drive in bad weather or squeeze their trucks into tight spots, like small garages or loading platforms.

Many over-the-road drivers not only drive, but also load and unload trucks. Others just drive. Both know, though, that their job is to deliver goods as quickly and safely as possible.

LOCAL CARTAGE DRIVER

While over-the-road drivers drive great distances, local cartage drivers drive only in a community, or local, area. They drive in the city and suburbs, but no farther. Local cartage drivers sometimes deliver packages from stores to people's homes. Or they may deliver bread from bakeries to grocery stores.

Local cartage drivers must know their way around the city. During the day they make many stops and meet a lot of people. Perhaps you have met a local cartage driver when he or she has rung the doorbell with a package for you.

OPERATIONS MANAGER

Trucking companies like to have their trucks running with a full load as often as possible. That way, the company that owns the trucks doesn't waste any of their valuable space. The operations manager makes sure that trucks are loaded all the time. He or she knows where all the company's trucks and drivers are and where they will be going.

The operations manager plans where trucks will go and when they should leave. He or she sets up times for packing and loading goods. The operations manager also lets customers know when a truck can come to their house to pick up their belongings.

The operations manager keeps track of the rates, or costs, for everything the company's trucks carry. He or she also helps decide what those rates should be.

DISPATCHER

The dispatcher is told by the operations manager where people are needed for the day's work. The dispatcher then tells drivers where they are to go. Every day, he or she gives the drivers the addresses of the houses or buildings where goods need to be packed and loaded. The dispatcher directs packers and helpers, too.

The dispatcher is also the trucking company's *weigh-master*. In this job, he or she weighs all the trucks that carry goods for delivery. The trucking company must know exactly how much weight its trucks carry. The dispatcher in the picture is noting the weight of a truck parked on a large scale.

ESTIMATOR

Families moving from one house to another must know how much it will cost to move their belongings. To give them an idea of the cost, the trucking company sends an estimator to their house. There, he or she checks the size and weight of what will be moved. Because the estimator knows how far the belongings must travel, he or she can make an *estimate* of how much it will cost to move. Distance and weight decide how much a trucking company will charge to move goods.

The estimator must be able to guess at the weight of many things. Since the estimator can't lift pianos and beds to see how heavy they are, he or she tries to tell their weight just by looking at their size. To do this job well takes lots of practice.

BUILDING MAINTENANCE MANAGER

A large trucking company's warehouse has millions of dollars worth of goods and equipment in it. To make sure that everything in the warehouse is safe, the building maintenance manager keeps the warehouse clean, heated, well lighted, and free of fire hazards.

Sometimes accidents happen in the warehouse. A forklift or truck may hit the large warehouse doors, for example. When this happens, the building maintenance manager repairs the damage. Outside the warehouse, the building maintenance manager can fix the large scale for weighing trucks if it breaks. A good building maintenance manager must be able to do many different jobs.

MECHANIC

The mechanic fixes trucks. When a truck does not work right, the mechanic finds out what is wrong and then corrects the problem. He or she is trained to know the parts of the truck, particularly its engine. Sometimes the mechanic replaces the bad parts with good ones.

While most cars have gasoline engines, trucks usually have *diesel* engines, which are cheaper to use. Trucking company mechanics can fix both gasoline and diesel engines. Mechanics must have special training to know how to fix diesel engines.

Before trucks leave the company's *terminal*, or parking and garage area, mechanics check them for fuel and oil. Mechanics make sure that the trucks are ready to make their trips safely.

PURCHASING DIRECTOR

Trucking companies need a lot of equipment. They need trucks and parts for fixing the trucks. They also need boxes and soft materials for packing, and much more. The purchasing director's job is to see that his or her company always has enough equipment and materials. The purchasing director, who often meets with salespersons, looks for the best prices. Then he or she buys what the company needs.

When new equipment arrives at the trucking company, the purchasing director checks to see that it is in good condition. It must be exactly what the company ordered.

The purchasing director also pays the company's bills. And when the company wants to borrow money to buy something—a new truck, for example—the purchasing director tries to arrange a loan with which to buy it.

CLAIMS DEPARTMENT MANAGER

Sometimes trucking companies break or lose the goods they move. When they do, they must pay to repair or replace the goods. The claims department manager talks to customers whose goods have been damaged or lost. He or she discusses how much money they should be paid for their losses.

The claims department manager inspects damaged goods. He or she knows about how much they were worth and tries to decide on a fair payment for the goods. The claims department manager must be a friendly person who can handle all kinds of complaints. He or she does not want customers to be unhappy with the trucking company's service.

ADVERTISING DIRECTOR

The advertising director tells people about the services that his or her company offers. To do this, he or she places *advertisements* in newspapers, magazines, and telephone books. The advertising director may also advertise on radio and television.

A trucking company's advertising director often attends meetings of other advertising directors. At the meetings, the advertising director explains what his or her company has to offer. And he or she listens to the ideas other companies have for making their business better.

To advertise their companies, advertising directors sometimes have toy trucks made, like the ones in the picture. Have you ever had a toy truck with the name of a real trucking company on it?

GENERAL MANAGER

The general manager makes all the trucking company's big decisions. He or she decides if the company should buy a new truck or build a new warehouse. The general manager also hires employees and tells them what their jobs are. He or she decides how much to pay each worker, too.

If somebody in the trucking company has a problem, he or she can see the general manager. The general manager wants to help all employees with their problems so that they can do their jobs well.

General managers have usually been in the trucking business for many years. They often learn to be managers by working at many of the jobs you have read about in this book.

Trucking careers described in this book

Warehouse Manager

Packer

Export Packer

Helper

Over-The-Road Driver

Local Cartage Driver

Operations Manager

Dispatcher

Estimator

Building Maintenance Manager

Mechanic

Purchasing Director

Claims Department Manager

Advertising Director

General Manager

A letter from a trucking company executive

United Van Lines Inc

Mohawk Transfer & Storage Co.
9721 James Avenue, So.
Minneapolis, Minnesota 55431

Dear Readers,

The moving business has changed a great deal since the time when teamsters of the Old West hitched up their horses to covered wagons and hauled goods across the country. We in the moving business today no longer use covered wagons, of course, but we always need the kind of hard-working people who used to drive them.

The people you have read about in this book know how satisfying it is to help move goods safely and quickly from one place to another, especially when the goods belong to a family that is moving. If you choose to work in trucking when you get older, you will know how satisfying it is, too.

Sincerely,

Herman Ladin
General Manager

The publisher would like to thank Mohawk Transfer Company and Mrs. Irving Fine for their cooperation in the preparation of this book.

The photographs in this book realistically depict existing conditions in the service or industry discussed, including the number of women and minority groups currently employed.

We specialize in publishing quality books for
young people. For a complete list please write

LERNER PUBLICATIONS COMPANY
241 First Avenue North, Minneapolis, Minnesota 55401